Ellis

BY

Andrew Joyce

Ellis

Softcover ISBN: 978-09981193-6-6

Published by William Birch & Assoc.

Dedicated To

Ellis Hodgkins

A man I deeply respect

Thanks to:

Emily Gmitter
The best editor in the world

Dr. Robert Bertagma

Johnny Oliver

Chris Wiberg

Wayne Hale

Austin Dorr

&

The town of Gloucester, Massachusetts

Act I

Prologue

Long after the mighty sheets of ice known as glaciers retreated back from whence they came, leaving the primeval stone of the island both smooth and scarred, the first of the Dorchester men landed at Half Moon Bay.

They did not last long. The land was not suited for farming. The dense forest precluded clearing land before winter descended upon them. And even if they had cleared the land, inches under the soil lay the pervasive granite that *was* the island.

Three years later, the men of Dorchester abandoned their short-lived colony and fled to nearby Naumkeag, which in later times would be known as Salem. However, within two generations, men were once again living on the island they came to call Gloucester. They named their county Essex after the Earl of Essex and they called themselves Gloucestermen. They were tried and true Englishmen.

In 1614, another Englishman by the name of John Smith, subsequent to his encounter with Pocahontas and while exploring the land he had named New England, came upon the island. He named it Tragabigzanda after a Turkish princess. However, at the request of Prince Charles, Smith renamed the island Cape Ann after the prince's mother, Anne of Denmark.

Rather than farm the land, the Gloucestermen farmed the trees of their island. They cleared great swaths of the forest for the building of sailing ships. They fished the bay for their sustenance, but did not venture far from shore. At least not in those days.

Years before Englishmen first set foot on the island that would one day be called Gloucester, the great schools of codfish of the George's Bank were known to the fearless explorers sent out by Queen Elizabeth. In fact, the cod were so plentiful along the New England coast that the Mariner Bartholomew Gosnold changed the name of Cape Saint James—a sandy peninsula he had explored in 1600—to Cape Cod.

In 1680, the men of Gloucester "went down to the sea in ships" to fish for cod in earnest. At first they fished the George's Bank, one hundred miles to the east. But in time, they made their way to the Grand Bank, one thousand miles from their home port.

By the early 18th century, it had become obvious that the ships they sailed were not ideal for fishing the numerous cod. The ships were slow and their holds could not contain enough salted fish to make the two-thousand-mile round-trip journey profitable.

In 1713, Captain Andrew Robinson designed and built a ship that had a larger hold for supplies and the multitude of fish he hoped to catch. Her sails were bigger and set higher to gather more wind. She was a two masted fore-and-aft rigged vessel. All the better to get to the banks faster and get home all the more quickly, where the cod could be sold before the other ships returned, hence getting the best price possible.

As she was being launched, a spectator exclaimed, "See how she scoons!" At the time, scooning was the act of skipping a flat rock upon the water.

In response, Captain Robinson shouted, "A schooner let her be!"

His schooner was an improvement over the fishing ships of the day and it was widely copied both here in America and in Europe. But it did have one flaw—it was top heavy. Between 1866 and 1890, three hundred and eighty schooners were lost at sea, taking 2,450 men to their watery graves. In one day, August 24, 1873, nine vessels, carrying one hundred and twenty-eight men, were lost over the Grand Banks.

In 1882, in an article published in the *Cape Ann Weekly Advertiser*, Captain Joseph Collins asked the rhetorical question, "When will the slaughter cease?"

Still the men of Gloucester went down to the sea in ships.

It was not until 1902, when Captain William Thomas commissioned a ship with a short deep hull and a rockered keel for stability, that fishing the Grand Banks became somewhat safer. The design was copied and used in the construction of fishing schooners until the days of sail were no longer.

Still the men of Gloucester went down to the sea in ships, but now their ships held no sails.

From this tradition—from this fearless and audacious heritage—came forth a man who would be the embodiment of the Gloucester fisherman.

Chapter One

The year was 1949. The boy was out of bed and getting dressed, even though the sun had not yet come up over in the East. It was summer, but there was a nip in the air.

This was the day. The day that the fourteen-year-old boy had looked forward to for weeks. He had saved the money he made from his paper route, delivering the *Gloucester Times*, to finance the adventure. He and his friend, Peter, had eagerly anticipated this day. For today, they were going to show the men how it was done.

Gloucester businesses were all about selling fish and outfitting fishermen, and involved mostly codfish. However, there was another fish that preyed the vast underwater banks of the North American continental shelf. This fish was worthless in the eyes of the Gloucester fishermen. The average weight of the fish ran about nine hundred pounds. It could take hours to land one of the monsters. And for what? Its flesh was worthless. You would be lucky to get three cents a pound after all your trouble. But the boy was bound and determined to land a bluefin tuna that day.

The path down the hill that led to the Ipswich River was well known to the boy. He had traversed it many times. The darkness did not impede his progress. There was a slight fog, but it only added to the mystique of what would be a magical day.

Peter was waiting for him at the river's edge. "I've got the bait and the hooks we bought last night. Did you bring your father's hand-line?" Without a word, the boy showed his right hand which held said object.

Silently, they climbed into the small skiff and shoved off. The boy sat at the bow with Peter aft. It was Peter's boat, so he had the honor of pulling the starting cord on the ten-horsepower outboard engine. The engine caught on the third pull and he sat down to steer the little boat downriver.

Although it was still dark out, there was enough ambient light for the boys to make their way through the marshes.

The occasional house they passed had its lights on. Soon the sun would drive out the darkness and they would have to share their world with others. But for the moment, they were the only two human beings extant on the planet.

The boy in the bow stared straight ahead and fidgeted with the hand-line. Peter knew not to speak when his friend was in deep thought.

The boy was thinking of the tuna he was setting out to kill. Did the tuna know he was coming? Did the tuna know this was to be its last day swimming in the cold waters of the North Atlantic?

The boy weighed ninety pounds. The tuna he was out to catch—with a hand-line nonetheless—might weigh a thousand pounds or more. It was just as likely that the tuna would pull the boy out of the skiff and drag him to the bottom of a very cold ocean and to his death. The boy figured it would be an even match. Let the best species win.

After an hour, they came to the mouth of the river and entered Ipswich Bay. They were headed for open sea. The bay was calm which meant the ocean would not be too bad. By now the sun had risen; its rays glistened on, and reflected off, the water. The boy raised his hand to shield his eyes from the brilliance as the small engine pushed him toward his destiny.

In due time, they were ten miles off the coast. It was time to fish.

They'd only enough money between them to buy three mackerel, so they would have to husband their bait *and* hope that a tuna did not snatch it and make off with it, leaving an empty hook. They had only three shots at the prize.

The boy baited the line as Peter looked on. This was the boy's show. Peter was only there to document the struggle and declare a winner ... whoever that may be.

The Atlantic is a mighty big ocean, bigger still if you're in a fourteen-foot boat. The expanse of nothingness that lies before you can be daunting to the most intrepid men of the sea.

The boy let out the line ... slowly ... three feet ... ten feet ... twenty feet ... forty feet. When the line hit the sixty-foot mark, he put on his gloves and sat down to await his fate. Would he return still a boy? Or would he return a man, trailing a thousand-pound tuna in his wake?

The day wore on. There was very little conversation between the two friends. The sun continued on its journey across a blue sky. Time was running out. They were only boys, they had to be home before dark or people would worry. The star we call our sun showed no mercy on that day as it moved across the sky at an alarming rate.

Late in the afternoon, the line jerked. The boy instinctively knew it was a bluefin. Through his gloves he felt the line running out to sea. It was a good feeling. He waited … he waited until he was sure. Then he jerked back on the line. He was almost pulled from the boat.

He had set the hook.

Now it was a waiting game. Darkness was fast approaching, but no matter. The boy would not return to Gloucester until he had won the battle.

The great tuna took off to the north. The boy held fast to the line. An hour later, the tuna turned east. The boy held fast to the line. His shoulders were aching. The line was wrapped around his hands, and despite the gloves, it stopped the flow of blood to his fingers. They were numb. Still he held on to the monster.

He thought of the great fish below the surface, fighting for its life, and he felt a pang of guilt. Did he have the right to take this beautiful creature's

11

life? That was his moment of doubt. He would have cut the line if doing so would have allowed the fish to live. But that was not the case. Even if he had cut the line … with a hook in its mouth and trailing sixty feet of line, the fish was already dead.

The boy set his jaw and said a silent prayer for the bluefin.

At length, his adversary tired. The bluefin had run for hours and now it was full dark. The boy pulled in his line. His hands were numb, his arms were on fire. The bluefin was dead. It had died from lack of oxygen. A bluefin must continuously swim for the oxygen-rich water to be forced through its gills.

The boys tied the fish to the stern and started the engine. They were going home.

They had been missed. The Coast Guard had been called out. The local fishermen cranked up their boats and were crisscrossing the bay looking for the wayward youths. Somehow, the little skiff made its way through all that activity and docked up the Ipswich River.

The boy found his fair share of trouble when the adults caught up with him. But he had caught his tuna … all 750 pounds of it.

Around Gloucester—from that day forward until he became an adult—he was known as "The Boy Wonder."

His name was Ellis Hodgkins and what follows is his story.

Chapter Two

Now that the war was over and Europe was on a stable footing, Ellis' Aunt Louise thought she would take a tour of the continent. In May of 1950, on a clear and sunny day, she set sail aboard the *Queen Mary*, heading east. Five days later, she arrived in Southampton, England, and proceeded to explore the British Isle from Edinburgh to Liverpool. Then she crossed the Channel and set about discovering the pleasures of France.

It was while in a sleepy little fishing village on the coast of France she came across a small sailboat. It was sixteen feet long, made of mahogany, had copper rivets, and sported brass rigging—a beautiful little boat. Louise immediately fell in love with it. After dickering with the owner, she bought it and had it shipped to the States in care of Ellis' parents.

The wooden crate arrived about two weeks after Aunt Louise's return to the United States, promptly stored in the family barn, and then just as promptly forgotten.

A year later, in the summer, Louise came for a visit. The Hodgkins homestead sat on a little rise overlooking Ipswich Bay, and Louise liked to sit on the front porch and look out at the sparkling waters of the bay. One morning, as the sixteen-year-old Ellis was preparing to leave for a day's adventure with his friends, Louise asked him to join her on the porch.

For a few moments, the two of them watched the morning sunlight dance on the water. Then, out of nowhere, his aunt asked Ellis if he could swim a hundred yards. He had never thought about it one way or the other. Of course, he could swim. But how long was a hundred yards anyway?

"Sure I can, Aunt Louise."

"I'll tell you what. If you can swim a hundred yards, I'll give you the sailboat sitting in the barn."

His summer vacation from school was just beginning, and Ellis thought that he'd love spending the warm summer days sailing the waters of Ipswich Bay.

"It's a deal," said Ellis with a crooked little smile on his face.

Ellis changed into his bathing suit and they went down to the beach. After measuring off the approximation of one hundred yards and setting up a marker, Ellis entered the water and swam out a certain distance. You see, Ellis, having been raised on the bay, knew its currents—at least the ones closest to shore.

When he felt the current pulling him, and with his aunt watching from shore, he began to swim. In no time at all he had passed the marker. As he was coming out of the water, Aunt Louise said, "I didn't know you could swim so fast."

Ellis had himself his first boat. He named her *Sea Devil*.

With the help of his father, he set the mast and installed the rigging. Then Ellis and a few friends carried the *Sea Devil* down to a cove on the bay. Now all he had to do was learn how to sail. In true Ellis form, he set out to teach himself. *Men have been doing it for thousands of years. It can't be that difficult.* And it wasn't—at least not for him. In no time at all, he was crisscrossing Ipswich Bay like an old salt.

For Ellis, sailing was a solitary endeavor. He felt free out on the bay, with the wind blowing through his hair and filling his sails. However, in time, his mother suggested he join the Ipswich Bay Yacht Club. "They hold races in the summer. You can compete with other boys and see how good you are compared to them."

His mother was partly right. The yacht club did hold races, but the "boys" Ellis raced against turned out to be closer to forty years of age ... men who had been sailing all their lives.

That first summer was rather demoralizing for the young sailor. He came in last or next to last in all his races. This prompted his mother to say, "You must do better. I cannot watch you go down in ignominious defeat every time you race."

Ellis had to agree on that point. It was no fun losing. But he never thought of quitting. Instead, he set about finding a solution to his problem. He knew he was a good sailor, at least as good as the men he competed against. But why did he always come in last?

Then one night, while he was lying in bed trying to fall asleep, it came to him. The problem was the sails! He had read an article in a sailing magazine a few days earlier about a new material called Dacron that was now being used for the making of

17

sails. Up to that point, sails were made of nylon, which had a tendency to stretch out over time. If sails are not taut and crisp, a boat cannot take advantage of the available wind to maximize its pushing power. Ellis needed new sails!

He made a few calls and heard about a guy over in Marblehead that had just set up shop making sails in his basement. His name was Ted Hood and word was he was a pretty decent sailmaker. Ellis called him and asked how much it would cost for a jib and main for his Town Class boat.

"I can do the job for $125 and have them for you by Friday, next week."

"I'll have to call you back. I have to ask my parents for the money."

"Sure, kid. Just let me know when you're ready."

Ellis relayed the information to his mother, who said, "You still have four more races in this season. It would be nice if you finished up there in the front of the pack at least once. Call Mr. Hood and tell him we'll pay him $150 if we can have the sails by Monday. You'll need a few days to practice with them before the race this weekend."

18

Mr. Hood readily agreed and Ellis had his sails in time for the next race. Ted Hood, by the way, went on to become the premier sailmaker in the world. His sails are used in the Americas Cup and any other sailing race of merit. His company has lofts in the USA, UK, Australia, Japan, and Argentina. However ... today, his sails go for a bit more than $125.

• • • • •

When the starting gun fires, the wind is blowing at twelve knots, coming in from the southwest. Nine boats jockey to be first over the starting line. Four make it before Ellis gets the *Sea Devil* over the line and onto the course. But that's alright. He's in the middle of the pack and not bringing up the rear as he usually does.

It's a four-mile course and there will be plenty of time to move up and overtake the competition. It will all come down to his skill at sailing. There are no more excuses. He has his new sails and his boat is just like every other boat out there.

The sun is to his back and hangs low in the sky. For the first half of the race they'll be heading into the wind, which will require a lot of tacking. That is where skill comes in. He'll have to bring the boat to the precise place on the water before he swings the tiller and tacks in the opposite direction. He has to keep his mainsheet in hand; there will be no tying off to a cleat in this race. He's going to keep that sail as taut as possible. The jib, he has tied tight. It will take care of itself—if Ellis knows his stuff. A sloppy tack will slow him down and he may end up back in his familiar position, bringing up the rear.

There are four boats ahead of him. His game plan is to sail against each one individually. He'll overtake them one at a time. Right now, he's focused on the boat just ahead of him. Nothing else exists on the planet but that boat. It had lost a bit of momentum during the last tack. *Good. Another tack like that and I'll pass him.* And he does. Now Ellis is in fourth place. But that sucks. His parents put out what was a lot of money for them, so he could be a competitor. And, by God, that's exactly what he's going to be.

Ellis looks out past the boats in front of him and sees that the ripples on the water have changed ever so slightly. The wind is changing direction by a few degrees. He ties off the mainsheet and pulls the jib in just a mite. Then he takes the mainsheet in his left hand. His right hand pushes the tiller a notch or two away from him. He is the first to take advantage of the wind change and passes the boat in front of him. He is now in third place.

They're coming up on the marker. When they round it, they'll be running with the wind—more or less. On the down leg, there'll be no tacking, only jibing. That's when you change your boat's direction with the stern and not the bow. It takes skill to do it right without losing momentum. Your boom must be amidships when you perform the maneuver, then you let it out just the right amount. And if you know what you're doing, you don't slow down one bit. And that day, Ellis knew what he was doing.

Ellis had become one with the *Sea Devil*. Together, they raced down that course and eventually passed the second place competitor. It was a glorious feeling. Now if he could just get out in front of the man ahead of him. But time ran out. If the course was only a hundred yards longer, he would have come in first. But coming in second was a heady feeling. He had lived up to his parents' faith in him.

• • • • •

Ellis won two of the remaining three races that season. And for the next four years, he was always

21

at the head of the pack when they crossed the finish line. He won more races than anyone else, and the races he didn't win, he came in second or third.

Sailing was not the only thing that held a young Ellis' attention in the summer of '51. There was also girls.

Over in the town of Boxford lived a comely lass by the name of Anne. She was a dark-haired beauty with piercing green eyes. Ellis had met her at one of his sailing regattas. She had batted her eyelashes in his general direction and he was hooked.

Anne was sixteen, as was Ellis. But she had a bit more experience. He was still a virgin … she was not.

"Why don't you come over and visit me this Saturday?" Anne asked coquettishly.

"I've got to practice my sailing," said a clueless Ellis.

Anne sighed. "My parents will be gone and I thought we might … well, you know."

Ellis was not *that* clueless. "What time?"

"Show up around ten. That will give us most of the day together."

On the appointed day, Ellis cranked up his '39 Ford convertible and headed over to Boxford. Anne was waiting for him on the porch.

Not a word was said. Anne took Ellis by the hand, led him into the house, and opened up a whole new world for him.

As he drove back to Ipswich, wearing a great big smile on his face, he thought, *That was fun. I think I might want to do some more of that.*

Ellis spent the next few years palling around with his friends, sailing, and pursuing the fairer sex.

But at the age of twenty-one, he had decided to change course. He sold his sailboat and moved to Gloucester. He wanted to try his hand at fishing for a living. It was a win-win as far as he was concerned. It would afford him the two things he loved more than anything else … being out on the water and competing, be it against himself or another man … or a fish. What was important was that he would be his own man and doing something that he loved. No working in an office for him.

He started out mating for some of the old-timers, and over the next two years, he learned his craft.

Chapter Three

By the age of twenty-three, Ellis had his own boat, the *Cape Ann*, and his own charter business, bringing wealthy men out to the banks for the sport of fighting and landing a bluefin tuna. By then, word had gotten around that if you wanted to test your mettle against nature, fighting a thousand-pound bluefin for two or three hours was one way to do it.

In those days, when the fish were still plentiful, Ellis was the man to see. He had an uncanny knack for knowing where the great fish swam in the warm summer months. Men came up from New York, men flocked in from the mainland of Massachusetts, they came down from Maine, and they flew in from America's heartland to hire Captain Ellis.

His fishing haunt was the Middle Bank, also known as Stellwagen Bank. Stellwagen is now a marine sanctuary, but back in the day it was Ellis' private fishing preserve. An apartment on T Wharf, overlooking the Rockport Inner Harbor, doubled as his base of operations for his charter business … and a house of ill repute when he was not fishing.

• • • • •

The incessant ringing awakens Ellis. However, before lifting the receiver, he glances at the clock sitting next to the phone, its luminescent hands throwing off a slight green glow. The time is 4:46 a.m. He had been asleep for less than an hour.

Groggily, and in a rasping whisper, Ellis speaks into the phone, "Hello?"

"Ellis, old buddy. It's me. Marty."

"Marty?"

"Yeah … Marty. Marty from Long Island. Me and my two buddies came up to do a little fishing."

Ellis' head clears a mite. He is wishing he had a glass of water. And a couple of aspirin wouldn't hurt either. He had spent a hard night of drinking a concoction invented by one of his friends. He did not know what it consisted of, but he did know the prime ingredient was rum … and a lot of it.

Before he can further respond to Marty, a voice next to him intrudes into the conversation. "Ellis, honey. What time is it?"

Oh yeah. I forgot about her, thinks Ellis.

"It's early. Go back to sleep."

From the phone comes a reply. "Damn right it's early. And we're already up here in Gloucester. We're going fishing. We have no plans to sleep until we've landed a bluefin."

"I wasn't speaking to you, Marty. Now tell me what the hell's going on."

"Ellis, I know I just woke you up from a sound sleep. So I'll make this easy for you. We're going fishing. You, me, Ted, and Verne."

"Ted and Verne?"

"Yeah! Ted and Verne, they're friends of mine. Now get your ass up. We'll be there in an hour. We're in an all-night diner just off Route 128 and just finishing breakfast."

Ellis is now fully awake. How dare this New Yorker call him in the middle of the night and demand he hop out of bed and take him fishing. Sure, Marty's a regular and a good customer. He's also a generous tipper when he catches fish. But still.

Then Ellis remembers that his coffers are at an all-time low. It's been a week since his last charter. Not because he didn't have the business, but because he's been too busy partying with his cronies and trying to bed every young female within the town limits of Rockport … and a few just over the town line.

Last night when they got low on rum, he had to make a call to the package store over in Gloucester. It went something like this:

"Hey, this is Ellis."

"Hi, Ellis. What can I do for you?"

"I need a half gallon of Bacardi, but I can't pay for it right now."

"No problem. It will be there in fifteen minutes."

"Thanks."

Everyone liked the Boy Wonder.

For financial reasons, Ellis had decided to take the charter, but he wasn't going to make it easy on ol' Marty.

Speaking into the phone, his voice now strong, he said, "What makes you think I don't already have a charter for the day?"

An eager Marty explains. "It doesn't matter. I'll pick up the full tab. I'm sure they'll let us tag along."

That's why Ellis liked Marty. He was an eternal optimist.

"Well, it just so happens that I'm free today, but you'll have to pick up the bait. Stop at Charlie Cucuro's fish house. You'll pass it on your way in. You can't miss it. It will be on your left, and there's a big red and white sign that you can see from the road."

"Will they be open this time of morning?"

"It's a fish house. They'll be open."

His conversation with Marty at an end, Ellis turns his attention to his bedmate. She's a comely lass who goes by the name of Susie. Her hair is long and blonde. She has a figure that just will not quit. He had met her the day before as the sun was making a spectacular descent behind the high hills in the west. The diminishing sunlight rippled in her hair as it does upon a wheat field in midsummer. She was a tourist up from Boston, walking T Wharf with her girlfriend.

Ellis had observed her from the vantage point of his second floor apartment and was smitten. He was soon standing next to the girls and introducing himself. He invited them up to his apartment for a cool drink, and called a friend to come over to entertain the girlfriend while he spoke with the blonde. Long after the rum had been delivered, the friend took the girlfriend home and Ellis was left alone with Susie.

One thing led to another and here they were.

Ellis leaned into her and gently kissed her cheek. She shifted in her sleep and smiled. He did not want to wake her. He would leave a note on the kitchen table telling her how much he had enjoyed meeting her and that he would be back sometime after sundown if she felt inclined to continue their escapades from the previous evening.

From the kitchen phone he called his mate, Wayne. "Come on, buddy. We got ourselves a charter."

"What do you mean *we*, white man?"

"I mean get your ass outta bed and meet me at the wharf in thirty minutes."

"Damn! I just hit the sack. Why didn't you tell me we had a charter today?"

"Look, Wayne, I didn't know it myself until ten minutes ago. We need the money, and thank God the fuel tanks are full. So, we're going."

"Okay, Captain. I'll see you at the wharf in half an hour."

The two men meet, climb down the ladder to their waiting dingy, and row out to the moored *Cape Ann*. As Wayne inspects the fishing tackle, Ellis brings the boat to life. At first she roars, but then settles down to a contented purr.

Wayne disengages the line tethering them to the mooring and Ellis deftly maneuvers the *Cape Ann* alongside the wharf. It is now almost 6:00 a.m. The sun is throwing a gentle light up and over the

31

eastern horizon, turning the sky a light gray as the clouds turn dark—almost black. But that would not last. Soon our star—our sun—would emerge in all her glory. The sky would turn orange, the clouds would rapidly turn from dark gray to purple, and then sing their joy as they became a vibrant pink. Glory hallelujah, the sun has risen! But all that means less than nothing to Ellis, his head is throbbing.

Marty and his friends arrive and soon the *Cape Ann* is headed due east, into the rising sun.

Ellis was not a religious man, not by a long shot. He might not have marveled at the majesty of God's sunrises, but he did have one ritual. Every time he took out a charter or just went out fishing for his own enjoyment, he would look to the south and see the concrete towers of Boston. And he would always say a silent prayer of thanks that he was out on the open ocean and not shackled to a desk in one of those monstrosities. The sea was Ellis' church.

After a little more than an hour, the boat slows; they are now over the Middle Bank. It's time to fish.

Wayne had rigged the gear on the way out. Each line hooked and baited.

The three New Yorkers stand at the stern and slowly let out their lines while Ellis keeps the boat steady and on course. It would not speak well of the captain if the lines were to tangle. After a hundred yards of line have been released, the anglers set their drags to fifty pounds and sit back—metaphorically speaking—to await the great bluefin tuna.

The minutes slowly pass … the hours drag on. Ellis thinks of Susie and her firm, round rear end. He keeps the fishing lines from tangling as he crisscrosses the bank in search of bluefin. The men down in the cockpit are swapping lies about the fish they had caught on previous outings and the women they had bedded in their younger days. Wayne sits in the small cabin wishing he was back in bed. He too had had a rough night.

Out of the depths, a bluefin strikes. Marty is the lucky one. It is his line running out to the south. Ellis slows the boat. Wayne comes alert. He yells to the other two men to reel in their lines—fast!

Ellis' headache is forgotten. Susie is forgotten. The only thing that matters now is landing the bluefin. It will be a two-man affair. Marty down in the cockpit and Ellis up on the fly bridge. The rest of the men on the boat have suddenly become superfluous.

Marty gives the fish some lead. Not much … just enough. Then he braces his knees against the transom. He has to do this right or the whole day will be for naught. He lets the fish run, thinking it had just scored a tasty morsel of mackerel.

Ellis says nothing. This is Marty's play. The boat is idling, but only momentarily. Once the hook is set, it will be Ellis' job to move the boat forward or to put her in reverse and move her backwards to keep Marty's line from getting tangled in the props. If the tuna takes off to the right or left and heads for the boat, Ellis will have to adjust his course. If the tuna pulls the line under the boat, it will be all over. Until the tuna is landed, he'll be working just as hard as Marty.

The reel is spinning at an alarming rate. The line is going straight out to sea. Twenty-five yards … fifty yards … seventy-five yards … wait … wait … NOW! Marty pulls back on the pole. BAM … the hook is set.

His friends slap him on the back and congratulate him. Ellis frowns and yells down to the men. "It's far from over. Give him room. Marty, you get in the chair, you've got a fight ahead of you. And Wayne, you know what to do. Stay behind the chair and don't let our customer get yanked out of the boat. We haven't been paid yet."

Ellis was thinking of a good friend of his, a charter captain by the name of Mike. It was just him and a single customer. There was no mate. A tuna hit, and the man sat down in the fighting chair with a big smile on his face. Mike was doing his delicate dance of keeping the line away from the props. He was in reverse when it happened. The tuna was a big one. Before Mike knew it, his customer was pulled from the chair and into the ocean. There was no time to react. The man was chewed up by the props and sunk to the bottom. A week later, a fishing trawler brought the body up in their nets.

Marty cranks the reel … he pulls back on the pole … he cranks again … he pulls again. At first it's exhilarating, thrilling … and so satisfying. But as time passes, his arms begin to ache. His feet are braced on the foot rest and his legs are on fire. Every muscle in his body is taut and tired.

If Ellis had not been fighting the fish in his own way from up on the fly bridge, the tuna would have pulled the boat miles out to sea. The process was simple. All they had to do was wear the fish out. Once it was exhausted, there'd be no problem reeling him in.

The adversaries are starting to get tired. But who will wear out first—the human or the fish? In a way, Marty was cheating. He had two diesel engines helping with the fight. The tuna had only its brute strength. The minutes wore on.

In a last ditch attempt to be rid of whatever was pulling him to his death, the tuna dives deep and heads straight for the boat. Ellis sees the line heading their way and gives the throttle a slight push forward. He has to keep the fish from the boat until it has no more fight left in him. Marty holds tight to the pole and cranks the reel. At this point, he just wants it to be over.

At the two hour-mark, the line goes slack. The tuna has given up. There is no fight left in him. He is on the verge of drowning because he cannot swim any longer. There is fear in his eyes … he knows he is going die. He is being pulled to what he does not know, but he does know that his days of swimming the cold Atlantic are at an end.

Up on the boat, Marty reels in the last few feet of line. The tuna rolls on the surface. He beholds the creatures that will take his life.

Wayne is there with the gaff. He hooks the tuna just behind the gills. This way the fish will bleed out and there will be just that much less blood to hose down off the deck when they return to port.

The tuna weighs six hundred pounds. So, naturally, no one is going to pull it up and over the gunwhale. Wayne sets up the gin pole, a contraption made up of a four by four and a block and tackle. It is the gin pole that will bring the tuna on board.

With the fish secured, everyone breathes a sigh of relief. Marty's buddies break out the beer. Marty sits back down in the chair, takes a deep pull from the cold brew, and accepts the accolades from his friends. Marty soaks it up. The praise is well earned.

Wayne stores the gear and gives Ellis the thumbs up. It's time to head for home. Another day, another dollar.

Ellis, from his perch high up on the fly bridge, nods to Wayne and puts her in gear. His course,

270 degrees—due west. Five minutes later, Ellis sees a large dark form, just under the surface, off the starboard bow. It's moving their way. He knows what it is and he cuts the engines.

They won the battle with the tuna. No way could they win against this creature.

The whale changes course and comes at the boat from amidships—starboard side. She's beautiful. Ellis is enthralled. If she continues on her current course, the boat will be nothing more than flotsam in a few minutes. And all on board will be sleeping in Davy Jones' locker this night.

On she comes. The men down in the cockpit are unaware of what is happening. They are swilling beer and laughing. Wayne is out of sight. He's most likely in the cabin, knocking down a beer himself.

Fine, thinks Ellis. *If we can come out here and kill a beautiful creature like a bluefin, then we should be fair game ourselves.*

On comes the whale.

Ellis braces for the collision.

Just short of the boat, the whale dives.

Ellis lets out his breath. He was not aware that he had been holding it.

He's about to restart the engines when the boat rises five feet into the air. The whale has come up under the *Cape Ann*. The lady whale is saying hello. She is a playful thing. A few seconds later, the boat has been gently deposited back onto the surface of the water. A giant tail, twenty feet off port, swishes in farewell.

Ellis grins, points the *Cape Ann* toward the setting sun, and shouts down below. "Wayne, bring me up a goddamn beer!"

Another day, another dollar.

Chapter Four

The wind is blowing at close to sixty knots. The sea is rolling—creating valleys twenty feet deep. The sheer walls of water would freeze a man's heart if he was unlucky enough to find himself at the bottom of one of those aqueous canyons. The freezing rain slants in almost horizontally, carrying with it chunks of hail that dimple the surface water. Spray from the whitecaps fills the frigid air with its salty fury.

• • • • •

Winters are harsh in New England and even harsher if you are out at sea. So Ellis looked around for something to keep him busy during those months and also put a few shekels in his pocket.

At the time, he drove an old Volkswagen beetle and liked the dependability of the car; so, he decided to become a Volkswagen salesman during the winter months while the *Cape Ann* was laid up in dry dock.

Ellis being Ellis, he had a demand when he applied for a job at the local dealership. "I'll work for you winter and spring, but come summer, I go fishing. If you can live with that, then we have a deal." His renown as a sport fisherman had preceded him. The local dealership enthusiastically put him to work selling cars.

Ellis earned the Top Salesman Plaque for six months running before leaving for a summer of fishing. Not a bad life for a twenty-five-year-old bachelor. It afforded him the time and means to pursue his two favorite sports—fishing and meeting young women. Not necessarily in that order.

As legendary as he was for his fishing acumen, Ellis was also celebrated—at least by the male population of Gloucester—for his way with the fairer sex.

There was the aforementioned Susie. Then there was Cindy, Fran, Terry, Elouise, Mary Beth, Diana … well, the list goes on. Their names alone would take up an entire chapter. This aspect of Ellis' "career" has been brought up for a reason. Because, while the women came and went, one name on the list belonged to one who had a profound effect on Ellis' life, but not in a way that he or anyone else could have ever imagined. Her name was Natalie. And her profession, at the time, was that of a nurse practitioner at Beverly Hospital.

· · · · ·

It's a beautiful January day. The sun is shining. Cottony white clouds race across an azure sky. The scarlet feathers of a lone cardinal stand out against the snow-covered branches of a stately oak—his morning song filling the cold, crisp air. The people of Gloucester are starting their day. God sits on his heavenly throne and smiles down on Cape Ann. He is pleased with his handiwork.

It is now the third winter since Ellis started selling cars. He is now the general manager of the dealership. The time is just a few minutes before 8:00 a.m. and Ellis is in his car heading for work. He's thinking of the night before and lamenting the fact that, for the first time in a long time, he had gone to bed alone.

I needed some rest anyway, reasons Ellis. Then he ruminates further. *Perhaps I'll call Sally after work and see if she wants to come over for a little dinner.* Now that he has that out of the way, he tries to turn his mind to more mundane matters, like helping his sales team sell a Volkswagen or two before day's end. But he can't help himself; a smile spreads across his face as he thinks, *If I ask her nicely, I wonder if Sally will wear her white mini-skirt this evening?*

The black Porsche 914 cuts the chilly air as it heads towards Ellis' fate. The car is moving with the flow of traffic—about sixty miles per hour—when suddenly and without warning, Ellis goes into an uncontrollable sneezing fit.

One sneeze after another in rapid-fire succession. And with each sneeze, Ellis' eyes close. At first, he's able to keep the car in its lane, but then, Fate intervenes. The right front tire hits a patch of black ice.

The Porsche skids to the right, across an empty driving lane, and heads directly for a sign post held up by two one-foot-square, solid steel I-beams. The ground in which they are imbedded is frozen solid. If a car were to hit either beam, there would be no forgiveness. It would be like hitting a brick wall, only worse. The wall would collapse … the beams are going nowhere.

Ellis sees his death fast approaching. There is no time to react. Just before impact, he thinks of

Sally. She knew how much he liked her in that white mini-skirt and he wonders if she will break with tradition and wear it to his funeral.

That is his last conscious thought before impact. The Porsche plows into the left I-beam and explodes into many pieces. Then there is only darkness.

A trucker hauling a load of lumber is the first to stop. He is a big, tough man. He had fought in the war with General Patton. He has seen death, but not like this. For the most part, they were clean deaths. A bullet hole and an exit wound. Even the men who had stepped on land mines were in relatively good shape. Yes, they were missing a leg or two, but you could still identify them by their face. Now, he is repulsed by what he sees and takes a step back.

There is nothing to be done. The poor son-of-a-bitch is obviously dead. He will wait until the police arrive, give his statement, get the hell out of there, and then stop at the first bar he sees. He needs a drink.

Thankfully, the cops soon arrive.

44

The first police officer on the scene has seen his fair share of accidents, but this one is something else. The car lies in pieces and the man who had been driving did not fare much better. The officer has radioed for an ambulance, but only as a matter of form. He should have called for a hearse.

It is rush hour and traffic is heavy. Drivers are slowing down to take a gander at the mayhem. The ambulance eventually arrives. As the paramedics approach the horrific scene, the cop fills them in on the details. The driver shrugs. He too has seen his fair share of death. He says to his partner, who is new on the job and still learning his way about, "Before we take him to the morgue, we have to confirm that he's dead."

Leaning into the destroyed car, the ambulance driver puts his stethoscope to the corpse's chest. "Goddamn! This man is alive!" he shouts.

The cop runs over. "Are you sure?"

"Sure I'm sure. He has a heartbeat!"

With great difficulty, the two attendants get Ellis—or what is left of him—onto the gurney. Once he is secured within the ambulance, the emergency lights are activated and the siren starts its woeful wail.

At the hospital, Ellis is rushed into an operating room where various liquids are pumped into his veins in an effort to stabilize him ... to keep him from going into shock and ultimately cardiac arrest. X-rays are taken and show that every bone in his head has been broken—all twenty-nine of 'em. His right leg has sustained breaks in twenty places. In short, Ellis is a mess.

However, the biggest mess is Ellis' face. Because of the trauma of the collision, it is twice its normal size. And with all those broken bones, the plastic surgeon that has been called in has no idea what the man looked like before the accident. How can he put him back together again if he doesn't know what he looked like before?

He mutters his predicament to the nurse standing next to him. She turns to him and says, "I've got a picture of him in my wallet. Will that help?"

"Go and get it."

Natalie runs to her locker and retrieves the cherished picture of Ellis that she has kept close since he gave it to her over a year ago. As she races back to the OR, she thinks, *That son-of-a-bitch is damn lucky I held on to this picture.* But she's smiling as she thinks it. Ellis was one of the kindest and most attentive lovers she had ever known.

Back in the OR, the doctors get down to the business of saving Ellis' life and reconstructing his face. Natalie is also there, doing her job. She is a professional, but still, a tear or two trickle down her cheeks. However, they are hidden by her surgical mask.

Besides everything else, Ellis was permanently blinded in his right eye.

It's twenty-four hours before he regains consciousness. His jaw is wired shut. He's wearing a cast from the hip down on his right leg. But he's having fun and holds court daily. His cop buddies from Gloucester smuggle in cocktails for him. His many girlfriends stop by—bringing flowers. His male friends can barely fit into the room because of all the women crowding around his bed.

A month later, he's discharged and walks out on two crutches. A month after that, he's using a cane, and the month after that, he's back at work.

No … not that kind of work. He's back to chasing anything wearing a skirt.

It's hard to keep a good man down. Just ask Natalie. She was the first person he called when he decided he had been celibate long enough.

In Ellis' mind, the whole affair was just another day in his life.

No big deal.

Chapter Five

In the year of our Lord, 1700, it's a gentle breeze that pushes the small sailing ship southwest, towards the northern coast of Cape Ann. The master and owner of the ship is John Lane who, together with his wife and children, is coming from Falmouth, Maine, after being run out by Indians during the First Indian War. It is a new century and a new beginning for the Lane family.

As the ship approaches land, John sees the dense forests he had been told about. His plan is to first clear a parcel in which to build their house. Then he and his sons will fell trees and sell the wood for the making of ships. There certainly is no shortage of raw material.

The ship anchors ten miles north of Gloucester Town, off Flatstone Cove. John and his eldest son, James, row a small dory to the shoreline. There is no beach, no soft white sand to set foot upon. The coast, as is the entire island, is made of granite. There is a small hill overlooking the cove, and it is there that Lane decides to build his house. The family will live onboard the boat until the house is inhabitable.

By 1704, John Lane had been given a grant of ten acres in and around the cove. It has been four years since the Lane family set foot upon the rocky shoreline. There were six children in the Lane clan when they landed, now there are nine. Before they are finished, John and his wife, Dorcas, will have brought a total of twelve new souls into the world. Not all of them will make it to adulthood, but enough of them do so. The land is eventually named Lanesville. And, in time, Flatstone Cove becomes known as Lane's Cove. So it went, generation after generation of Lanes populating the northern region of the island known as Cape Ann.

• • • • •

The year: 1974. The place: Cape Ann Marina.

Ellis and Wayne have just come in from a day of tuna fishing. The men who had chartered the *Cape Ann* for the day are a happy lot. They got themselves a tuna—almost 800 pounds. By now, the Japanese had discovered the tuna-rich fishing grounds off Gloucester. And any fish they could not catch themselves, they bought from the local fishermen. The price had risen from the three cents of Ellis' youth to six dollars per pound. There's a lot of sushi sold in Japan.

After having taken numerous pictures with their prize, Ellis' customers gave him the tuna, as a tip, to dispose of as he saw fit. He sold it to a Japanese buyer for $4,800—without having to leave the dock. He split the cash with Wayne and headed over to the bar.

Everybody in Gloucester knew Ellis, and that included all the people in the bar that evening. It took him a few minutes to respond to all the salutations he received as he walked through the door. It was a big room and he had to make the rounds, shaking hands with the men and winking at the women. Luckily, the barmaid knew his poison, and it was waiting for him when he finally sat down on the barstool.

He sipped his drink slowly. It was early and he was wound up from the day's adventures. He thought he'd have one more drink and then order dinner. After that, he'd see how things panned out. It had been a good day. And with money in his pocket and a gleam in his eye, he was looking to make it a good night as well.

As Ellis sat on his stool contemplating his drink and looking in the mirror behind the bar, a vision of loveliness caught his eye. She had legs that just would not quit. Her hair was auburn, her eyes green, and her smile brought joy to the hearts of men. She was a direct descendant of John Lane.

"Who's that girl?" he asked the barmaid.

"She's the new waitress."

"Why haven't I seen her before?"

"Probably because she's the *new* waitress," came the sarcastic reply.

"You know what I mean. I know every female on this island between the ages of eighteen and twenty-five and I've never seen her before. What's her name?"

"It's Laura … something. Wait. Now I remember—it's Laura Lane."

"Where is she from?"

"Jeeze, Ellis. You want her phone number and bra size too? I was just introduced to her when I came on shift. You can do your own dirty work. I got drinks to serve."

The young barmaid walked away in a huff. Probably because she was an ex-lover of the man who was asking all the questions about another woman.

Ellis moved to the end of the bar, to the serving area where the waitresses picked up their drink orders. It was a safe bet he'd be able to get in a few words while the beauty was waiting for her orders to be filled.

He let her come and go twice before he said anything. He was letting the line run out. On her third trip back, after she had just placed an order for two vodka martinis on the rocks and a draft beer, Ellis tried to set the hook.

"Hi. My name's Ellis. I've been watching you and I gotta say that you are sensational. I'm not trying to hit on you or anything. I just want you to know that I think you are beautiful."

The girl smiled, and her eyes grew wide. "I know who you are. Everybody knows who you are."

Ellis thought, *This is going to be easy.* But before he could go on with his spiel, the girl continued. "And everyone knows that you are the horniest hound dog around. You've bedded three of my girlfriends that I know of, but ... I must admit ... they all speak quite highly of you. And that's amazing, seeing as how you dumped each one of them after a few romps in the sack."

Just then her order was placed before her. She put the drinks on a small tray and departed without saying another word.

The hook had not been fully set.

Well, it may not be that *easy,* thought Ellis. *But it might be a lot of fun trying.*

When she came back, Ellis asked, "Wanna have dinner with me some night?"

In spite of herself, Laura was attracted to the smiling man who looked straight into her eyes. After she gave her drink order to the barmaid, she said, "If dinner is all you have in mind, then I see no reason to decline your kind offer."

"That's great. When is your next night off?"

"I'm off Mondays and Tuesdays. Take your pick."

"I think Monday is the best day of the week to sit down to dinner with a beautiful woman."

Laura blushed at the compliment. She wrote her phone number on a bar napkin and handed it to Ellis. "Call me Monday afternoon to confirm. For all I know, you'll be entangled with some other woman by then."

With a light laugh, Ellis replied, "Don't worry. I'll fit you in somehow."

Laura rolled her eyes and said, "I would appreciate that considerably," before leaving with her drink order.

Monday finally rolled around, and Ellis, after having called to ascertain the address and confirm that he was still looking forward to seeing her, was at Laura's apartment at eight on the dot.

Ellis held the car door open for her. As she slid in, he once again appreciated her long legs. He took her to a small and intimate place on Rogers Street, owned by a friend of his. Out back there was an enclosed garden with one table—"Ellis' Table." When Ellis walked through the door with Laura, the proprietor welcomed him as a long-lost friend and escorted them to Ellis' private dining room.

It was a warm summer night and the scent of flowers filled the air. Colorful Japanese lanterns adorned the walls of the garden and soft music emanated from unseen speakers. No menus were presented, only a bottle of crisp, dry white wine.

While the waiter uncorked the bottle, Ellis said, "I hope you don't mind, but I called ahead and ordered our dinner. And I hope you like white wine. I'm not big on the red stuff. But you can have whatever you'd like."

"No, white is fine. What's for dinner?"

"Why not be surprised?"

Laura consented to be surprised and shyly sipped her wine.

Ellis had downed his wine in two gulps. He was a little nervous. He raised the wine bottle out of the ice bucket and refilled his glass.

"Okay. Now that we have that out of the way, tell me about yourself."

Looking at Ellis from over the rim of her wine glass, Laura countered, "Most men like to talk about themselves. Why don't you go first?"

"You've already told me that you knew all about me. I'm the horny hound dog, remember? So, I'd like to know a little something about you. For instance, how long have you lived in Gloucester? Where do you come from? And how did you get to be so goddamn beautiful?"

Laura put her glass down and thought for a moment before answering.

This guy's on the make alright. This place would soften up any woman. Stay on your toes, Laura girl. He's just asking about you to put you off your guard. I have to admit, he's done everything right so far. But just remember that he only wants to get into your pants. Enjoy the meal, enjoy your night out, and then have him drive you straight home. No going over to his place for a nightcap.

"Well, Ellis, I've only lived in this part of Gloucester for a few weeks now. But I was born on the island. In fact, my family has been on Gloucester since the year 1700. You ever been up to Lanesville?"

57

"Many times."

"That's where I'm from."

"Why haven't I ever seen you before?"

"Probably because you don't hang out at high schools all that much. You're about ten years older than I am. When I was in school, you were down here doing your fishing ... for both tuna—and the way I hear it—women. When I graduated high school, I went off to college. I'm home for the summer now, but there's no work up in Lanesville or the vicinity. I thought it would be cool to come to Gloucester and get a job. I didn't want to commute, so I got myself an apartment down here. It's small but cozy. There you have it. My whole life story."

Ellis refilled her glass and said, "Not quite."

"What do you mean?"

"You haven't told me how you got to be so goddamn beautiful."

Laura laughed and said, "You're too much, Ellis." Ellis tilted his wine glass toward her in a silent toast and said, "I try to be." Then they talked

58

about this and they talked about that. Small talk mostly, until dinner was served. During dinner, Ellis confessed that his family had also settled in the area during the 1700s. "But a little later than yours. I think it was about 1750 or thereabouts."

They lingered over dinner, enjoying the food, the company, and the conversation.

On the way back to Laura's apartment, Ellis was talkative, but did not mention stopping by his apartment for a nightcap or anything of that sort. He asked questions about her family history and seemed genuinely interested in her answers. At her place, he again opened the car door for her and escorted her to her apartment.

Here it comes, she thought. *He's going to ask to come in "for just a little while."*

However, he did no such thing. Instead, he held out his hand and shook hers, saying, "I've had a wonderful evening, Laura, and I've enjoyed your company. Goodnight."

With a perplexed look on her face, Laura watched Ellis' retreating figure as he descended the stairs.

He didn't even try *to kiss me goodnight. Maybe I was wrong about him. Either that or he didn't like me.*

She got out her key and let herself into the apartment. After making sure the door was locked, she leaned against it and was stunned to realize she was a little disappointed that Ellis had not made a move on her.

Chapter Six

Five days went by before Laura heard from Ellis again. It was over the phone that he asked her, "Tomorrow is Monday and I was wondering if you'd like to shoot a little pool?"

Laura smiled into the phone before answering. *He's interested in me after all.*

"I don't know how to play pool."

"Neither do I. So don't worry about it. There's an Irish pub right down the block from you. Perhaps you've seen the green and white sign. The name's Mulroney's."

"I've seen the sign, but I've never been in there."

"They also have dartboards and they make the best hamburgers in town. If you're free, I thought we could meet there about seven-ish. We could play a few racks and throw a few darts while drinking draft Guinness. Then we'll have us some hamburgers and call it an early night. I've got a charter Tuesday morning."

"Sounds like it might be fun. I'll see you tomorrow."

They met at the prescribed time, played the aforementioned games, and consumed said beer and burgers. In the course of the evening, they got to know one another on a slightly deeper level. Even though things were lighthearted, or maybe because no one was trying to impress anyone, they let their true selves show through. And they both liked what they saw.

Ellis was quiet as he walked Laura back to her place. He hadn't meant to feel this way. At first he was just out to bed a beautiful woman. And that was all. But a monkey wrench had been thrown into the mix. She had turned out to be more than a set of long legs and a pretty face.

She's smart and fun to be around and so much more. This one, Ellis old buddy, you've got to treat a little differently. You've got to show a little respect.

"What are you thinking about, Ellis?"

"I was just thinking. Seeing as how you've got the day off, I was wondering if you'd like to come over to my place tomorrow night and have dinner.

I haven't told you before, but I'm a gourmet cook. I'll dazzle you with my cooking."

If it had not been for the first two dates with Ellis where he behaved as a perfect gentleman, Laura would have declined the invitation. But now ... she wasn't so sure she would mind Ellis getting into her pants.

"Sounds like fun. What time?"

"We dine at eight. I live on T Wharf over in Rockport. There's a long staircase on the outside of the building going up to my place. You can't miss it. But if you do, just ask anyone to point the way to Captain Ellis. You'll find me."

At her door, Ellis did not ask to come in ... or shake her hand. He leaned into her and gave her a kiss on the cheek and then he was gone.

Ellis had some work to do before the next night. Rockport was a dry town. That meant no bars, no liquor stores, no nothing. Hence, his apartment became the *de facto* place to hang out at night. There was always a crowd. The young guys came to have a few drinks and watch the Celtics or Bruins play. Or if the season was right, the Boston Patriots. The young girls came because that's where the boys were. There was a party happening every night up in his apartment, regardless if Ellis was there or not.

He passed the word around that his apartment was off limits for one night. If anyone felt the need to hang out, they could drive down to Gloucester. It was only ten minutes away.

Laura showed up a few minutes after eight. Ellis met her at the door with his signature smile. "Please come in. Did you have any trouble finding me?"

"Nope. You're right where you said you'd be."

He sat her on the couch and said, "I'll be right back."

He came back holding two glasses of wine, one of which he held out to Laura.

"Thank you," she said.

Ellis sat down on the couch, but not right next to Laura. He sat at the other end so that he could turn sideways and look at her as they spoke.

They sipped their wine in silence for a few minutes, and then Laura asked, "What's for dinner?"

"I want to surprise you again."

"Do you need any help?"

"No, thank you. I've got it covered."

Laura looked around the apartment, and just for something to say, remarked, "Nice place you've got here."

"Yeah. I had to pay one of the neighborhood girls to clean it while I was out fishing today. I didn't want you to see me in my natural habitat."

She laughed nervously. She was feeling differently toward Ellis. She couldn't quite put her finger on it. But then it dawned on her. *What if he doesn't make a pass at me tonight? How am I going to feel about that?*

Being the straightforward type, she decided to get it out in the open before dinner. She could deal with whatever the answer was, but she wanted it out of the way before she ate or else the food would lay heavy in her stomach. No matter how good it was.

She steeled herself, took a deep swallow of wine, and then blurted out, "What's the matter with me?"

Ellis was taken aback. "As far as I can see, nothing."

"I mean, why haven't you tried to talk me out of my clothes?"

"Do you want me to talk you out of your clothes?"

"Yes. I mean, no! But it would help my ego if you'd at least try."

Ellis smiled a crooked smile and put his wine glass down on the coffee table. He moved over and took the glass out of her hand and placed it next to his. He touched her cheek with the back of his hand and said, "I've held off because you're special."

Looking into her bottomless green eyes, he leaned over and softly ... gently ... kissed her. She responded. All their pent-up inhibitions dissipated as they caressed one another. They were free. Ellis

66

whispered in her ear, "The hell with it." He stood and scooped her off the couch and carried her to his bedroom. Still holding her in his arms, he kicked the bedroom door closed with his right foot.

Two hours later, they walked out of the bedroom … faces aglow with contentment. Laura sat on the couch while Ellis went to retrieve the bottle of wine. Once their glasses were replenished, Laura inquired, "I suppose your dinner is ruined by now."

"Not by a longshot."

Ellis reached for the phone sitting on the coffee table. With the receiver in hand, he dialed a number from memory. "Hello. Tony's Pizza? This is Captain Ellis. I'd like the large deluxe, the one with everything on it. Of course, with anchovies."

When he had finished with Tony's, Ellis lifted his glass toward Laura and said, "Here's to you, Beautiful."

"Not so fast, *Captain* Ellis. Didn't you promise me a gourmet meal?"

"I promised you a dinner. I said I was a gourmet cook, but I lied. What are you gonna do about it?"

"This is what."

Still holding her glass, Laura wrapped her arms around Ellis' neck—spilling a little wine in the process—and gave him a great big kiss right on the lips.

"What are you going to do about *that*?" she wanted to know.

"As soon as we get the pizza out of the way, I'll show you."

The summer of '74 was the time that Ellis came the closest to being hooked, reeled in, and put on display. Even though their schedules were different—he worked days, she nights—they spent as much time together as possible.

During the days that Ellis had no charter, he'd take Laura out on the *Cape Ann* ostensibly to teach her to fish. However, very little fishing was ever attempted. Laura always packed a picnic lunch and Ellis brought a cooler of beer. They would anchor a few miles out and enjoy each other's company, the warm sun on their bodies, and the vast expanse of blue ocean that lay before them. Those were idyllic days.

A few years back, a woman had spied Ellis walking out of a restaurant and approached him. "Hello. My name is Patty Sullivan and I'm kind of a talent coordinator. Have you ever thought of modeling?"

Ellis grinned and said, "You gotta be kidding me."

"No, I'm not. I can get you what's called catalogue work. Most male models are what I call soft-handsome. You have a rugged look about you. You'd be perfect for catalogues that are selling manly items. Like hunting gear, cars, that sort of thing."

"How much does it pay?"

"By industry standards, not a whole lot. But it's still more than the average Joe makes in a day. Besides, it's not hard work. All you've got to do is stand there and look ruggedly handsome."

What the hell? It might be fun, thought Ellis. He agreed to give it a shot as long as it didn't interfere with his charter business.

That's how Ellis became a model, and modeling is what landed Ellis a spot as an extra in a film starring Liza Minelli and directed by Otto Preminger. The movie was called *Tell Me You Love Me, Julie Moon.*

When Ellis got the call from Patty asking him if he was interested in playing a man sitting at a table in a restaurant while the stars of the movie cavorted around him, he had two questions: "How much does it pay? And can my girl be in it too?"

"It pays a little more than you'd get for a day's modeling. And I'm told the shoot shouldn't take more than two hours. But it could go on longer. As to your second question, I had to send over your picture to the movie people for their approval. But knowing you, Ellis, I'm sure the girl is a knockout. So I'll set it up."

Ellis only agreed to participate because he thought Laura would get a kick out of it. It would give her something interesting to tell her friends about when she went back to college in the fall. Little did he suspect that *he* would dominate her conversations with her girlfriends when she returned to school.

By happenstance, the part of the movie that Ellis and Laura were to be in was being filmed at *The Blacksmith Shop* restaurant located right next door to Ellis' apartment. A crew member seated them at a table on an aisle. They were told to look like they were in a deep conversation as the camera was wheeled past them. The setup was that the camera would go down the aisle and end up taking a shot of the harbor through a big plate glass window at the back of the restaurant.

As people ran around setting up for the shot, making sure the lighting was perfect, that the microphone was set properly, and all the other things that go into making a movie, Ellis noticed that where he was sitting the aisle was a little narrower than the rest of the walkway. The camera wouldn't fit through the gap. So, Ellis being Ellis, he stood up and moved the table back a foot or two.

You would have thought he was guilty of kidnapping the Lindbergh baby, killing Cock Robin, and any other number of sundry and forbidden things.

Otto Preminger came storming down the aisle, yelling and screaming. "Don't you dare touch anything! You do nothing unless I tell you!" And

71

on and on he went. He moved the table back to its original position and with a final omniscient glare in Ellis' direction, stomped off to his director's chair.

Ellis said nothing. When the tirade was over, he looked across the table at Laura and winked.

Eventually, the camera operator was ready, the sound man was ready, the movie stars were ready, and most importantly, Mr. Otto was ready.

"Action!" yelled the director.

The camera started on its way down the aisle. When it got to Ellis' table, its movement was halted. It couldn't fit through the gap between the tables. Ellis shrugged and Laura laughed. Preminger sent the assistant director to move the table back to where Ellis had placed it, and the filming resumed with no further mishaps.

Laura quit her job in late August so she could spend more time with Ellis before she had to go back to college. Ellis thought that was just dandy and whisked her off for a romantic week in Bermuda. While on the island, Laura broached the subject of continuing the relationship while she was away.

They were walking along the beach, holding hands. The water was topaz-blue, the white sand scrunched under their feet, the sunlight warmed the two lovers as Laura began to speak. "This summer has been the best time of my life, Ellis. What do you think? Do you want to keep it going? We can write each other and keep in touch. I'll be back in just a few months for Thanksgiving and Christmas. Maybe you could come to Lanesville and meet my parents."

Ellis tightened his grip on her hand. He had a deep affection for the beautiful redhead walking next to him. She was wonderful. She was intelligent, fun to be with, a sensual lover, and best of all, she laughed at his lame jokes as though she really found them funny.

He sighed and told her the truth. "Baby, you are the best. You can have any man you want and I am so flattered that you want to be with me. But I'm not the marrying kind. I like you too much to bullshit you. We've had a wonderful summer and I will always remember it. In later years, when you're surrounded by your children and grandchildren, I'll have only my memories of this summer … and of you. I'll never forget you and I'll always love you. But you have to steer a different course than the one I'm on. To come onboard with me would only break your heart in the long run. Can you understand that?"

Laura looked into Ellis's eyes and saw the love he had for her. A love that would let her go rather than lie to her. A love that treated her as an equal, a love that was profound and perhaps never ending.

It was now Laura's turn to sigh. "When I am surrounded by all those kids and grandkids, and even though my husband will be standing next to me, within my heart there will be a small place for you and this wonderful summer that you have given me."

When they returned to Gloucester, Laura spent one last night with Ellis. They made slow and sweet love all night long, knowing that it was to be the last time.

The next morning, Laura said her final good-bye to Ellis.

He never saw her again.

Chapter Seven

"Hello. Is this Ellis Hodgkins?"

"Who wants to know?"

"My name is Dan Levin. I'm a writer for Sports Illustrated."

"Sure you are."

"Seriously. We would like to feature you in an upcoming issue."

"Why in hell would you want to do that?"

"Word has come to us about your prowess when hunting the bluefin tuna. We're planning an article about the demise of the fishing grounds and seeing as how you were the one who kind of got the whole thing started, my editor and I thought you'd be the person to talk to. It's as simple as that."

"How did you hear about me?"

"We have a mutual friend by the name of Myron Birch. He's been telling me about the legend of

Captain Ellis for a while now. I finally did a little research into you, and lo and behold, he wasn't shitting me. So what do you say? You wanna be written up in a big-time magazine?"

"I'll have to think on it. Give me your phone number and I'll call you back."

Ellis was pretty sure the phone call was a put-up job instigated by one of his friends. However, the number did have a New York City area code. He called back later that day and was a bit surprised when a professional-sounding woman answered. "Time, Inc. How may I direct your call?"

"I'd like to speak with Dan Levin."

"Yes, sir."

A moment later, Ellis was speaking to Levin, "I guess you're legit. How do you want to do this?"

Three weeks later, Levin and a photographer from Sports Illustrated met with Ellis at the Cape Ann Marina.

Levin spoke first. "Mr. Hodgkins, this is Peter Balasko. He's my photographer. The plan is that we will follow you around for a week. I'll be asking you questions and Pete will be taking pictures. How does that sound to you?"

Ellis had one question he needed answered before things went any further. "Who's picking up the bar tab tonight?"

"We're on an expense account, Mr. Hodgkins. Wherever you go for the next week is on us."

Ellis smiled and said, "So what do you want to know?"

"We're here to learn about you and bluefin tuna fishing. While researching you, I came across an article written in the *Gloucester Times*. It was about the time when you were fourteen and you caught a 750-pound tuna with a hand line. Why don't you tell me about that and then we'll progress from there."

"I had forgotten all about that."

"You forgot that you landed a 750 pound tuna?"

"No … I forgot about it being written up in the newspaper."

So, the men from New York stayed a week in Gloucester. Besides interviewing Ellis and people who knew him, at night they would follow Ellis to his favorite haunts and sit at a nearby table listening in on the talk of the Cape Ann fisherman and his friends. They never overtly intruded into his life, and for that Ellis was grateful. For his part, he never took advantage of the Sports Illustrated purse. Even though they picked up the tab everywhere he went that week, Ellis was restrained in his ordering. He bought a round for the house only once.

Levin gathered what information he could and Balasko took pictures he deemed appropriate for the article. Two months later, it appeared in the November 18th, 1974 issue of Sports Illustrated magazine.

The lead sentence read as follows: *Ellis Hodgkins stands in his doorway, huddled against the wind, squinting out to sea with his one good eye.*

When the article came out, everyone in town loved it and hailed Ellis as a hero—everyone, that is, except his mother. She did not like the fact that it mentioned he had only one good eye.

"Why did you let them write that about your bad eye?" inquired his mother.

"I had no say in it. And besides, who cares?" answered Ellis.

That was Ellis. He had one rule that he lived by. It was a simple rule. He never broke it and he never strayed from its fundamental precept. To quote Ellis, "Who gives a fuck?" Or as stated in his high school year book: *The Boy Least Likely to Give a Good Gosh Darn*. It was 1953 after all. That was as explicit as they could get.

One thing all the Sports Illustrated hoopla brought home to bear, at least for Ellis, was the fact that the days of catching bluefin tuna—at least in the way he had done it—were over. The article made note that Ellis' charters had gone from one hundred eighty-two catches of bluefin in one season to thirteen within a three-year span. It was time to move on.

He put his boat up for sale and informed the owner of the Volkswagen dealership that he was leaving town. It was nothing personal, but he was looking for new horizons. And besides, he had grown tired of the car business. He gave a two-month notice. His last day would be July 4th.

Ellis was an employee any boss would want to keep around. He had once suggested that the dealership should stay open on Christmas Eve.

"Maybe we can sell a car or two."

"I can't get any of the salesmen to stay here on Christmas Eve," replied the owner.

"No need to. I'll do it. You never know. Maybe someone will want to buy a car for a last-minute Christmas gift."

Shaking his head at the dedication of his employee, the owner said, "Forget it, Ellis."

A little while later, when Ellis started to get restless and make noises like he might be ready to move on to another profession, the owner handed him a blank check and told him to go get himself a boat. Ellis had sold the original *Cape Ann* the previous fall.

"Go and do a little fishing and then come back."

"How much do I spend?"

"Just get a boat that you like, catch yourself some damn fish, and then come back here and sell some cars for me."

Now, two years later, here was Ellis announcing he was *definitely* leaving, but the owner didn't think anyone being paid as much as Ellis was would ever give up that kind of money. For the next sixty days, every time he saw Ellis, he would say, "You're not leaving." And every time Ellis would respond, "Yes, I am."

On July 3rd, his boss observed him packing up his things and said to Ellis in a resigned voice, "I guess you *are* leaving."

"I guess I am," responded Ellis.

In the hopes that he would return, the dealership sent him a paycheck every week for one year *and* they kept him on their insurance program for the same amount of time. Ellis would call his ex-boss periodically and implore him to stop sending the checks. However, they kept coming every week for fifty-two weeks straight. Even long after Ellis had moved far from Gloucester.

His many friends and acquaintances threw him a going-away party, the likes of which were seldom seen in that neck of the woods. It was a massive affair—standing room only. Half the town showed up. Two days later, he packed up his conversion van and his current lady friend, Karla, and headed south.

Act II of Ellis' life was about to start.

Act II

Chapter Eight

His village sits at the mouth of the Touloukaera
River. Touloukaera means *life giving* in the
Tequesta language. Aichi is awake early this
morn. It is still dark as he paddles his canoe across
the short expanse of water that leads to the barrier
island to the east.

Today he will build three fires on the beach for the
purpose of giving thanks to *Tamosi*, The Ancient
One—the God of his people. The fires must be lit
before the dawn arrives. It has been a bountiful
season. The men have caught many fish and killed
many deer. The women of his village gathered
enough palmetto berries, palm nuts, and coco
plums to last until next season. There is an
abundance of coontie root for the making of flour.
Tomosi has been good to his people.

Tonight, the entire village will honor *Tomosi*. But
this morning, Aichi will honor Him in a solitary
way. Because tonight, at the celebration, he will
wed Aloi, the most beautiful woman in the village.
It took many seasons to win her heart, and now he

must acknowledge *Tomosi's* role in having Aloi fall in love with him.

He builds three fires to represent man's three souls—the eyes, the shadow, and the reflection. When the fires are burning bright and the flames are leaping into the cool morning air in an effort to reach *Tomosi*, Aichi will face the ocean. With the fires behind him, he'll kneel on the fine white sand and lower his head until his forehead meets the earth. He will then start to pray and will continue with his prayers until the sun rises out of the eastern sea. At that time, he will ask that he be shown an omen that his prayers have been heard.

The first rays of the awakened sun reflects off the white sand. Aichi raises his head and there before him is the sign *Tomosi* has sent him. Not a mile away, floating on the calm, blue ocean are three canoes of great size. He can see men walking on what looks like huts. He knows they are sent from *Tomosi* because they each have squares of white fluttering in the light breeze. White denotes The Ancient One. And if that were not enough, no men paddle the massive canoes. They are moving under their own power, traveling north to the land where *Tomosi* lives. The men upon those canoes must not be men at all. They are the souls of the dead being taken to the heaven of the righteous.

Aichi leaps to his feet and runs along the shoreline trying to keep abreast of the canoes. But in time, he falls behind and soon they drop below the horizon. What a wondrous day this is. He has communed with his god and tonight he will wed Aloi. With joy in his heart, Aichi runs back to his canoe. He must tell the people of his village what he has seen.

What Aichi has seen are not spirit canoes. They are three ships from the fleet commanded by Juan Ponce de León. He is sailing along the coast of a peninsula he has named *Florido* which means "full of flowers." He is in search of gold to bring back to his king. He has also heard from the Indians to the south that somewhere to the north lies a natural spring that confers eternal youth to those who drink from its cool, clear waters. To bring a cask of that water back to Spain would make him a rich man indeed. The year is 1513 A.D.

Aichi and Aloi produce many children and grandchildren. But to no avail. The coming of the Spaniards has decimated the Tequesta. Most have died of the diseases brought by the white man. Others were captured and sold into slavery. By the year 1750, the village by the river that celebrated

Tomosi's largess in the year 1513 is abandoned and overgrown with plant life.

In the spring of 1788, the Spanish drive the Creek and Oconee Indians south to the land once populated by the Tequesta. The Spanish refer to the bands of Indians as Cimarrons, which means Wild Ones. The Americans to the north bastardize the name and call the Indians, Seminoles.

In 1789, a band of Seminoles, tired of running from the Spanish, inhabit the place on the river where the Tequesta once lived. They name the river, *Himmarasee*, meaning "New Water." They live in relative peace for twenty-seven years. But at the outbreak of The First Seminole War, the Seminoles move their village farther west and into the Everglades to keep out of the white man's reach.

In 1821, Spain cedes Florida to the United States, and the Americans begin surveying and mapping their new territory. Over time, the shifting sands of the barrier island caused the mouth of the river to empty into the Atlantic Ocean at different points along the coast. As the coastline was periodically charted, the surveyors—not understanding the effects of the shifting sand on the river's behavior—thought that the various entry points were "new" rivers; hence, each time the land was surveyed, the map makers would make the notation "new river" on the updated chart.

The 1830 census lists seventy people living in and around the "New River Settlement."

In the year 1838, at the beginning of The Second Seminole War, Major William Lauderdale and his Tennessee Volunteers are ordered to build a stockade to protect the settlers along what has become known as The New River. He selects a location of firm and level ground at the mouth of the river where once the Tequesta and Seminoles had built their villages.

The fort is decommissioned after only a few months. Two months later, the Seminoles burn it to the ground. The fort is now gone, but the name remains.

There are no roads into Fort Lauderdale until 1892, when a single road linking Miami to the south and Lantana to the north is cut out of the mangroves. In 1911, Fort Lauderdale is incorporated into a city.

During the 1920s, there is a land boom in South Florida. Everybody and his brother is buying land.

When the most desired land runs out, developers make acres of new land by dredging the waterways and using the sand and silt thus obtained to make islands where future houses will one day stand.

Because of its natural geography and the dredging that went on in the '20s, Fort Lauderdale has become known as the American Venice. There are countless canals, both large and small. Most houses on those canals have a boat tied up behind it. And many of those who do not live on a canal have boats sitting in marinas or sitting on a trailer in their backyards.

In 1974, twelve percent of the population of Broward County, in which Fort Lauderdale lies, makes a direct living off the boating industry. Another twenty percent benefits indirectly.

Into this world Ellis Hodgkins descends ... trailing Karla in his wake.

Chapter Nine

In 1975, at the site on the New River where Aichi and Aloi were wed, where the Seminoles had built their village before retreating into the Everglades, and where William Lauderdale built his fort, Ellis sits in a condo unit up on the sixteenth floor, in air-conditioned comfort. He has arrived in Fort Lauderdale. Now what the hell is he going to do?

The apartment was owned by a friend who offered its use to Ellis until he could secure his own living accommodations. The friend, a wealthy manufacturer of fishing equipment, lived in New York, so Ellis had the place to himself. Well, Karla was there, but he didn't mind sharing it with her—especially when she came up from sunning herself at the pool, wearing that skimpy white bikini. She was *definitely* a pleasure to have around.

Two weeks later, Ellis and Karla were living in their own place, a small apartment building just off the beach. Ellis knew people from all around the world who were connected to the fishing and boating industries, and Fort Lauderdale was no exception. During the day, he would go around and visit various people he knew, primarily those who worked at boat dealerships, and inform them that he had relocated to Fort Lauderdale and was looking for work as a captain.

He had a full captain's license that allowed him to carry passengers for hire anywhere in the continental United States. At the time that was kind of unusual—if not downright unheard of. In those days, a captain's license was good for only certain areas. For instance, if your license was issued for Cape Cod, you would be authorized to work anywhere within a one-hundred-mile radius of Cape Cod. But Ellis got one for the entire territorial waters of the United States. However, first he had to pass the test. And for that, he had to have a little help.

• • • • •

Six months earlier:

Patty: Come on, Ellis. You have to know this stuff for the test.

Ellis: Can't we fool around first?

Patty: No! Now be a good boy and tell me ... when you're coming up on a marker that has a green light on it, what side do you go to?

Ellis: Port.

Patty: Both international and inland, the rules require that a stand-on vessel shall take action to avoid collision when she determines that _____?

Ellis: Aw, come on, Patty. We've been doing this forever. I know the answers and I'll ace the test tomorrow. But right now, I just want you over here, sitting on my lap.

Patty: Answer the question first.

Ellis: A collision cannot be avoided by the give-way vessel's maneuver alone.

Patty: Very good. Now, where did you want me?

The next day, bright and early, Ellis was at the Boston Coast Guard Station on Atlantic Avenue.

The man in charge was Commander Mallett.

Commander Mallett: You passed the test with a score of 96, which is rather exceptional. Congratulations.

Ellis: Thank you, sir.

Commander Mallett: What are your plans?

Ellis: I'm going down to Florida and I thought I'd like to captain a boat or two.

Commander Mallett: You know, your license is good for only in and around Gloucester.

Ellis: Can I have it transferred to Florida?

Commander Mallett: What part of Florida?

Ellis: The Fort Lauderdale area.

Commander Mallett: I'll tell you what. My wife and I are retiring down there next year. I'll issue you a license that is good for all the United States' territorial waters. These licenses are very rare. In exchange, you take us out for a boat ride when we get down there.

And that is how Ellis got his captain's license.

• • • • •

One of the places Ellis went to spread the word of his availability for employment was a Hatteras dealership. He knew a woman there by the name of Claire.

"Hi, Claire. I just hit town and I'm looking for work. You know anybody who might need a captain?"

"Ellis, you old son-of-a-bitch. Good to see you."

The long and short of it was that the dealership had just sold a 58' Hatteras to a Canadian gentleman and he was looking for someone to captain it for him.

Ellis got the job and moved onto the boat. Karla had been homesick and had departed for the North the previous week.

It was a good job. The family came down maybe three times a year. The rest of the time, Ellis maintained the boat and had it ready to go at a moment's notice in case the owner called from Canada and said, "I'll be there in a few hours and I'm bringing guests with me. Have her gassed up." The owner also invited Ellis to use the boat whenever he wanted. "Take it out on occasion. Do a little fishing."

On one of his forays, Ellis took out a few friends and twenty young ladies. It was quite the party. The girls were scantily clad and everyone was having a ball. On the way back in, the marina manager saw the boat with the bevy of beauties and promptly called the owner to report Ellis' outrageous behavior.

"Did you know that your captain threw a party on your boat? And he took it out filled with people?"

"Did they look like they were having fun?"

"I'd say. There were young girls from stem to stern."

"Well, if they were having a good time, that's all that matters. And in the future, I'd thank you to mind your own business."

The owner's name was Michael Gobuty. He was from Winnipeg, Canada, and he was a good man to work for.

Ellis made friends easily. Especially of the female variety. He always had a ready crew at hand. The girls brought plenty of food and would divvy up the jobs before leaving the dock. When they returned from the sea, they got right to work cleaning the boat. It was quite a sight. All those young girls in their bikinis washing and polishing while Ellis sat up on the fly bridge sipping beer, seemingly with not a care in the world. He was the envy of the marina (except for the manager).

One time, the owner's wife came into town unexpectedly. She, of course, slept in the master stateroom. Ellis had his own quarters in the bow. Well, Ellis had met a sweet little thing the night before and had brought her home, not knowing the wife was in town.

The next morning, the wife had a mild shock when she got out of bed and saw a nude girl in the galley making coffee. The wife, whose name was Denise, was a good sport about it. Her only comment: "Ellis, can you have your lady friends cover up? What if the children had been here?"

The "children" of whom she spoke were her two boys, both in their early teens. Ellis very politely made the observation that maybe the kids wouldn't mind all that much finding a nude woman on their boat. But in a serious tone, he promised to instill a strict dress code among his "crew members." One that would be adhered to at all times.

Two years later, Mr. Gobuty decided to upgrade his sea-going experience. He bought a larger boat—a sixty-eight-foot Roamer. But that meant the old boat had to be sold. Ellis put it on the market and waited for the fish to nibble.

The first fish to come along was Julio Iglesias. Yes, *that* Julio Iglesias. At the height of his career. This was before the internet. The ad was running in the local newspaper and the boat was listed for $500,000. As Ellis was showing Julio around, he discerned that the man was hot to trot to buy the boat. After showing him everything, the engine room, the staterooms, how the windless worked—everything—they retired to the main salon.

"I really like this boat. She's a fine lady," said Julio.

"Yes, we've maintained her well," responded Ellis.

Julio took out his checkbook. "So the price is $500,000?"

"I'm sorry, Mr. Iglesias, but that was a misprint in the paper. The actual sale price is $550,000."

It wasn't a misprint. Ellis knew the boat was worth the extra $50,000 to Julio, and Mr. Gobuty has been a good boss, so why not make him a present of the extra $50,000?

Julio smiled. "No problem. But there's just one thing. Can you stick around for a week or two until I find a captain?"

"I'll have to ask Mr. Gobuty. But I don't think that will be a problem."

"Here's a check for the full amount."

Ellis and Julio became friends as Ellis showed Julio how to run the boat. They went out fishing a few times and shared more than a beer or two while tied up at the dock behind Julio's house in Miami. One day, around sunset, after an exceptionally good fishing day, Julio pointed to his house (it was more like a mansion) and said, "I have a full-time cook, three full-time housekeepers, a butler, and God knows what else. I'm practically never here, and tomorrow I have to jet off to France for a concert. Then it's on to Germany. I've really enjoyed fishing with you and I appreciated your patience while teaching me the ways of seamanship and boating."

Ellis nodded and said, "You were an apt student. It's been my pleasure."

Julio beamed at the compliment. "Anyway, I was thinking that you should throw a party for your friends. My pantry's full and I got more booze than I know what to do with. I'll tell my people that you have the run of the whole house. Go wild. Consider it a tip."

"That's nice of you, Julio. But I think I'll go back up to Fort Lauderdale. Mr. Gobuty's new boat is going to be delivered any day now and I have to be on hand for that."

The new boat was named the *Rahji*. One day, Ellis was on the fly bridge, watching the world go by, when a couple came down the dock and stopped in front of the boat. "Do you remember me?" asked the man.

"I sure do. You're Commander Mallett," said Ellis as he came down the ladder and jumped onto the dock. He shook the commander's hand, then said, "And this lovely lady must be your wife."

With the niceties out of the way, Ellis asked them if they were ready to go for their boat ride.

"You mean right now?" asked Mallett. "Do you have the time?"

"Even if I didn't, I'd make the time for you. That license you gave me is a wonder. When I go in to get it renewed, I get a low whistle from whoever is in charge. And I'm told the same thing every year."

"What's that?"

"That it's very valuable and I should not let it expire because it would be very difficult to replace."

Ellis escorted Mr. and Mrs. Mallett on board and cast off the lines. He took them up the Intercoastal Waterway and showed them the sights in and around Fort Lauderdale. On the way back, they stopped at a waterfront restaurant and Ellis sprang for a late lunch.

By and large, Ellis had a lot of free time on his hands. The Gobutys came down only a few times a year and stayed for a week or so. At other times, business associates of Mr. Gobuty would stay on the boat for a few days, taking in a little fishing. But that was it. The rest of the time, Ellis had to himself.

After four years of captaining for the Gobutys, he cast his good eye about, looking for something to keep him busy *and* put a few coins in his pocket. Then he hit on it. He went from marina to marina, asking the proprietors one specific question: "If a boat needs engine work, how does the owner get it to the marina for repairs?" He was trying to learn if there was an outfit that would tow a non-running boat to their marina. This was in the days before mobile mechanics came on the scene.

When he had ascertained that there was no one towing boats from people's homes to marinas, he called Mr. Gobuty.

"Hello, Michael."

"Hello, Ellis. What's up?"

"I was wondering if you'd mind if I started a little business on the side. I thought I'd go into the boat towing business. I won't let it interfere with my duties for you."

"Go for it, Ellis. Do you need any help financially to get the show off the ground?"

"I'm cool, Michael … and thanks."

Ellis got himself a little twenty-two-foot boat, had some cards printed up, and passed them out at all the marinas in Fort Lauderdale. And there are a lot of marinas in Fort Lauderdale.

Before he knew it, he was ferrying boats all over the place.

Chapter Ten

Ellis named his towing business Cape Ann Towing and his tow boat the *Cape Ann*. The endeavor started out small. Back in those days, the Coast Guard would tow a disabled boat to its home port. However, as Ellis' business began to take hold, the policy was changed. They would still tow you in, but only to the nearest port of call. After that, it was up to the boat owner to get the boat to its home berth. That's where Ellis came in. Being the only game in town, Cape Ann Towing grew fast. But Ellis' first allegiance was always to Mr. Gobuty and the *Rahji*.

Two years later, Mr. Gobuty informed Ellis that he had sold the *Rahji*. "I just don't get enough use out of it. But you've been a good captain and a good friend. I want you to find an apartment on the water where you can keep your tow boat tied up and I'll pay the first six months' rent. Also, there's a credit at the marina of $3,500 and I instructed the manager to turn it over to you."

The moment was bittersweet for Ellis. He loved his job, but now he would be free to build up his business. There had been many jobs he'd had to turn down while the Gobutys or their friends were in town. And he could see that just over the horizon, he'd have competition. There were too many boats and too many towing jobs in the Fort Lauderdale area for someone else not to get the same bright idea.

His first boat, the twenty-two-footer, was sufficient for what he started out doing: Towing boats from a person's home dock to a marina for repairs, or towing in the occasional fisherman stranded a few miles out at sea. However, Ellis was starting to get calls to tow larger and larger boats.

Fort Lauderdale has tight waterways, with the currents mostly unpredictable from place to place. And the New River with its twists and turns, not to mention its extensive boat traffic, made plying those waters while towing a boat a nightmare … or an accident waiting to happen. It was time to get a second boat and hire some help.

Ellis found himself a 31' Bertram and a helper, whom he promptly schooled in the ways of towing. Now, for the larger vessels, there were two tow boats. Ellis captained the *Cape Ann II* in the bow boat while the *Cape Ann I* was piloted by the captain in the tail boat. They kept in contact by radio because they couldn't see one another.

Eventually some competition did come along. But it was a friendly competition in the form of a guy named Red Koch. He and Ellis became drinking buddies and would help one another out if one of them had a particularly hard tow. Sometimes three boats were needed for the large mega yachts. The insurance companies required that they be towed up—or down—the New River. There was so much that could go wrong along a river with so many turns and so many expensive boats tied up along its sides.

Speaking of insurance ... with all that could go wrong while towing a boat, Ellis's insurance bill was $15,000 a year. And that was in 1970s dollars!

It was about this time in his life that Ellis stopped drinking. He kept a marine radio in his car and another one in his house. He listened to it 24/7, never knowing when he was going to be called out on a tow job. And sometimes lives were at stake. Hence, he decided he had drunk his fill for one lifetime. It was time to grow up.

There were lighter moments in the towing business. For instance, the time Ellis tied up to a boat and started towing. After a while, he thought to himself, *This is an easy tow. There's no drag.* Then he turned to see the boat floating in the middle of the waterway, about a hundred yards back. The tow line had slipped off.

Or the time he was doing a bank repo. As he was tying the line to the boat, a neighbor came running out, shouting all over the place that it was his friend's boat that Ellis was taking and he would not allow it. To which Ellis replied, "This is a legal repossession. If you have a problem with that, I can call the cops on my radio and have you arrested for interfering with bank business and anything else that cops can think up."

"That's okay. Take the boat. He's not that good a friend."

Once, Ellis was called up to Stuart, Florida, which is about a hundred miles north of Fort Lauderdale. He was to tow a 40' Hatteras down to Miami for repairs. The owner said he just couldn't get it started. No problem for Ellis. A long tow like that paid very well.

107

About halfway to Miami, Ellis' boat conked out and he couldn't get it restarted. He was using only one boat at the time. He was sitting there in the middle of the Intercoastal Waterway with boats passing him on all sides. Then the current got a hold of him. He looked around for a place to anchor or tie up or anything else that would help him out of the dire situation he found himself in. There was nothing. If he dropped his anchor, he would have been right in the middle of all the boat traffic that just happened to be around at that inopportune moment. Besides, the boat he was towing would have swung out and hit some damn fool that got too close. Wouldn't you know it? It was a Sunday and everybody and his brother was out on the water that day.

Ellis did not lose his head as some men might have. He looked to the boat floating twenty feet aft of his disabled vessel and shrugged. *Why not?* He pulled the tow line in and jumped onto the Hatteras.

With a silent prayer he turned the keys. To his great relief, both engines fired right up. He continued to Miami using the Hatteras as his tow boat. He still billed the owner in full. He had gotten the Hatteras to Miami … and that's what he had been contracted to do.

108

Ellis always charged cash. He had a healthy aversion to checks. As you're towing someone from a disaster, be it small or great, they are your best friend. But when they're safely tied up to their home dock, some will forget your name real fast. If his client had no cash with him at the time, Ellis would take a radio or GPS as collateral, which were usually worth much more than his towing fee. Almost everyone ran Ellis down the next day with a handful of cash. Ellis got stung very few times during his towing career.

One time, he was towing one of those mega yachts up the river, and when they got to where they were going, Ellis yelled up to the captain, "That'll be $2,000."

"One minute, I'll send the mate back with the cash."

Ellis' boat was nudged up to the transom of the yacht. When the mate appeared holding a bundle of bills, Ellis sent *his* mate up to the bow to get the cash. Something went wrong with the hand-off. The next thing Ellis knew, there were twenty, one-hundred-dollar bills floating on the wind—swirling here and there. And one by one, they dropped onto the murky water of the New River where the current swiftly swept them away.

There were no recriminations, no yelling about whose fault it was. The mate for the yacht smiled and said, "I'll go and get another stack." Yachts of that size always kept large amounts of cash on hand for the buying of supplies and emergencies. And $2,000 blowing away *was* an emergency of sorts.

Coast Guard boats seldom broke down, but if they did, the crews would politely refuse all offers of assistance from the general public. They did not want to be seen being towed in by a civilian. Captain Ellis was the exception. There were a few times that they readily accepted his offer to get them to their home port.

It wasn't long before Ellis was well-known among the Coast Guard, the Florida Marine Patrol, and the local cops. And that played well for a few of the local smugglers. Ellis did not know about it until years later, but eventually he was informed concerning his unintentional complicity in marijuana smuggling.

"Hey, Ellis. We want to thank you for all the help you gave us with bringing in those tons and tons of marijuana."

"What are you taking about? I don't like drugs. I don't do drugs and I won't allow drugs anywhere near me!"

"Remember back when we were calling you for a tow on an almost weekly basis?"

"I remember. I made a lot of money off you dumb asses. You should have had your engines overhauled."

"Well, Ellis, this is the way it worked. We would get a load right up to the Florida coast. When we were a few miles offshore, we'd shut off our engines and radio you to come to our rescue. And you would show up and tow us in. On the way, we always passed some coppers, be it Coast Guard or local. Because they all knew you, they waved us on. If we had been under our own steam, we probably would have been stopped and boarded at least ninety percent of the time. We'd still be in jail. So, thanks, Old Buddy."

Another story that kind of concerns smuggling is the time Ellis sold a boat that had been impounded by the Coast Guard. It went down something like this.

The boat had gone aground on one of the sandbars at the mouth of the New River. It sat there for a few days before the Coast Guard came out to investigate.

They got there and discovered that the boat was filled to the gunwales with pot. Whoever had brought the load in had the smarts to "bale" (pun intended) when the boat went aground. Their boss probably had them killed later, but that's another story.

The Coast Guard called Ellis to get the boat free and tow it to a marina that they used for storing impounded boats. He got it there and the marina people hauled it out of the water and put it up on blocks. The Feds came and off-loaded the contraband and went on their merry way.

Of course, they tried to find the owner. But the last registered owner said he had sold the boat months before. He gave the Feds the name of the person he sold it to, showing them the paperwork on the sale, but if that person existed, the Feds could not find him.

So there the boat sat. Because they had no one to prosecute, the Feds were in no hurry to pay the marina or Ellis for their services. It looked like

Ellis was going to have to sue the Federal Government to get paid. The owner of the marina didn't care all that much because he had a plethora of boats the Feds were paying on. He figured he'd just eat this one and chalk it up to doing business with the Federal Government. But Ellis wasn't doing a lot of business with them and he wanted his money.

Well, one day, Ellis was hanging around the marina when this guy came up to him and asked, "What's the deal on that boat? Is it for sale? She sure is a beauty." He was referring to the pot boat.

Without missing a beat, Ellis said, "It might be for sale. What do you have in mind?"

"I live in New Jersey and I got a trailer that will carry it. I sure would like to take it home with me."

"It has no paperwork, no registration, no nothing. Are you cool with that?"

"I'm from New Jersey. I can get paperwork for it."

"Fine, then it's yours for $8,000 cash."

With cash in hand, Ellis had the boat loaded on the man's trailer, paid the marina their share, and pocketed the rest. He was well paid for that one particular tow. The Feds never asked about it and to this day probably don't know it's missing. Well … now they do. But the statute of limitations has long since run out.

It was inevitable that Ellis' towing activities would lead him to his next endeavor—raising sunken boats.

One of his first calls was to raise a 36' Sea Ray.

"Hello, is this Cape Ann Towing?"

"Yes, it is. How may I help you?"

"Do you raise sunken boats?"

Ellis had to think about it for a moment. *Why not?* "Tell me where the boat is and we'll come out and take a look at it."

"How much do you charge?"

"I'll tell you after I see the job."

The reason Ellis was not forthcoming with a price is because he had no idea what to charge. After hanging up, he called an insurance adjuster he knew and asked what the going rate was for bringing up a boat.

"If it's at dockside ... about a hundred dollars a foot."

"Sounds good to me. Thanks."

Ellis arrived at the job with no equipment but a small gasoline pump and two tools known as come-alongs. He and his helper attached the come-alongs to the pilings and worked at getting the boat out of the mud and its gunwales just above the water.

Then Ellis threw the pump hose onboard and cranked up the pump. The boat came up pretty as you please. And like a sea serpent, she looked around and rapidly went back down below the waves. He eventually got her up and she stayed up. In time, Ellis was the go-to guy if you needed a boat refloated from the murky depths.

In the beginning, if he got a call late at night, he'd tell the person, "We'll be there first thing in the morning." Then he'd show up the next morning and the boat would be floating on the water when it should have been resting down in Davey Jones' locker.

"What happened?" demanded Ellis.

"My friends and I worked all night and got her up. I'm sorry you came out here for nothing."

After three or four times of that, Ellis always told the caller, "We're on our way. We'll have your boat up in no time at all." He never again lost another refloating job to well-meaning amateurs.

Ellis did his towing and refloating thing for about twenty years. Then one day, he decided to call it quits. He had come to town in an old van and with very little money. He did have Karla with him, so that was a plus. He also had many friends in the boating industry because of his reputation as a fisherman. By the time he sold his towing business, he had many more friends. Like up in Gloucester, he had become a local legend. But this time it was because of his towing and boat refloating activities and accomplishments.

He sold the goodwill of Cape Ann Towing and its name for $500,000 cash. The tow boats he kept. Ellis had always been sentimental about boats.

116

Time to begin Act III.

Act III

Chapter Eleven

Ellis' Act III is still unfolding, but this is how it's played out so far.

Besides boats, there was one other thing Ellis has always been sentimental about, and that is women. He had never married because he figured there were too many women in the world to limit himself to just one. He has always been an honest man, so cheating was out of the question. Hence, no marriage for Ellis.

He bought himself a 48' Californian to live on. Of course, he named her *Cape Ann*. She's a beautiful boat. The staterooms are on multiple levels. The main stateroom is one level down from the salon. The walls are covered in rich, dark teak. The galley is spacious and stocked with all the appliances any kitchen should have. In ten years, Ellis has not once used the oven. Ellis does not cook and never has.

Even though Ellis is now retired, he still doesn't drink. But he likes to frequent restaurants that double as sports bars. He's a rabid Patriots fan and the same goes for the Miami Heat. One of his favorite places to go and watch the games is a local Hooters. He goes there most nights for dinner and, as a result, has gotten to know the staff quite well.

A few years ago, the girls of Hooters put together a calendar featuring their favorite customers. Ellis was Mr. April.

He's so popular with the girls that they worry about him. They're always running by his boat bringing care packages of food. And they take turns cleaning it for him. They did those things because they like the guy, not for money. But Ellis had to put his foot down.

"Look, girls. I appreciate the food and the cleaning service, but I'm gonna have to lock you out unless you start taking payment. You girls work hard at your job and I can afford to pay you for services rendered. You're saving me a lot of trips to the grocery store, and I don't have to go out and hire a cleaning woman."

Arrangements were made and now Ellis has the best-looking cleaning crew and food delivery service in all of Fort Lauderdale.

He has always been a car enthusiast. The front page of the October 11, 1974 edition of the local Gloucester paper featured a picture of a smiling Ellis, standing next to a brand new Briclin. A Briclin was an American-made car that looked like a cross between a Corvette and a DeLorean. It was way ahead of its time. It had gull-wing doors and safety features that would not be introduced in other American cars for another decade. The point being that Ellis has always had an eye for cars. In his time, he's owned well over a hundred ... so far.

One of his favorite cars was a 1968 red GTO. It was in mint condition, and Ellis had owned it only a few weeks when, in a sense, it was taken away from him.

He was driving on one of the main drags when a car started following him. The driver started honking his horn and the passenger was waving her arm out the window. They were trying to get his attention ... and they succeeded.

Ellis shook his head. *It's always something.* He pulled into a parking lot and got out of his car and waited. The other car pulled up behind him and a man and woman got out. *If this is going to be a fight, then it's not fair. Two against one!*

The man reached into his coat pocket, and Ellis went on high alert. But it was not a gun or knife the guy was reaching for; instead, he pulled out a business card.

Handing the card to Ellis, the man said, "I'm with Castle Rock Entertainment. Is that a '68 GTO?"

Ellis was always getting smiles and thumbs up about the car. He was used to that, but being pulled off the road was a bit much. However, he, as always, was polite. "Yes, it's a '68," he said and turned to leave.

"Wait! You don't understand. We want to rent it. We're making a movie and your car would be perfect in a few of the scenes."

That stopped Ellis in his tracks. He had just bought the car for $9,000. If he could get a little of that back by renting it out for a few days, why not? Besides, it would be kind of cool to see his car in a movie.

"How much are you figuring on paying me to use this beautiful, classic machine in your movie?"

"The going rate is $700 a day. Right now I don't know how many days we'll need it. That's up to the director. And he's going to have to okay the car. Can you bring it by our office tomorrow and let him see it? If he likes it, we can sign the paperwork then. The address is on my card."

"I assume you guys are insured."

"To the hilt."

"By the way. What's the name of the movie?"

"*Striptease*. It stars Demi Moore and Burt Reynolds."

"Okay. I'll see you tomorrow. What time?"

"Make it about ten-ish."

The director loved the car and made a deal on the spot. In fact, he loved the car so much, he kept it for the duration of the shoot. When Ellis went to pick it up, he was given a check for a little over $9,000. He had not driven it much, but it had already paid for itself.

As he was getting ready to leave the parking lot where the production company had its offices, a guy walked up him and asked if that was the car being used in the movie.

"It is, but now it's retired."

"I'll give you $10,500 for it right now. I gotta have that car."

Ellis shrugged. *What the hell?* He couldn't turn down the money. He could have, but he wasn't impressed that the car had been in a movie. Hell, he had been in a movie and he wasn't all that impressed with himself. Besides, there were a lot of '68 GTOs out there.

Ellis was still dating and most of the women were a bit younger than he was. One day he's sitting in the main salon on his boat and he's thinking, *There's a lot of wasted space here.* Ellis isn't big on furniture, so the space *was* kind of wide open. Then it hit him. He knew exactly what the salon needed.

He called a guy that worked in stainless steel. Boats have a lot of stainless steel on them and, as stated before, Ellis knew everyone.

He brought the man to the salon and asked him if he could fabricate and install a piece of stainless steel tubing running from the floor to the ceiling.

"Where do you want it?"

126

"In the middle of the room would be nice."

"What do you want it for?"

"It's going to be a stripper's pole."

"In that case, there'll be no charge."

The first girl he brought home after the installation asked what that pole was doing in the middle of his living room.

He had an idea that she knew what it was. "That wouldn't interest you."

"How do you know?"

"It's a stripper's pole."

The girl went over, placed her hand on the pole, and swayed just a little bit. Ellis said nothing.

"Do you have any music, Ellis?"

"There's a radio over there. Help yourself."

After she had selected a hard rock station, she went back to the pole and wrapped her arms around it.

A nonchalant and magnanimous Ellis said, "Okay … if you want to try it out, be my guest."

That was the beginning of Ellis' private strip club.

As I was interviewing people for this book, a narrative emerged: Everyone I spoke with loved Ellis. Not one person said a bad word against the man. So, I had to ask him: "Why does everyone like you so much?"

"I treat people with respect," was his simple but profound answer.

I had one more question to ask.

"Ellis, how would you sum up your life?"

"I've lived a very enjoyable life perusing endeavors that were legal and that rewarded me well. I have been able to enjoy my lifestyle—which was not extravagant—to its fullest."

If only we all could say the same thing. Ellis is now eighty-two years old and still going strong.

Although the stripper pole doesn't get the workout it once did.

About the Author

Andrew Joyce left high school at seventeen to hitchhike throughout the US, Canada, and Mexico. He wouldn't return from his journey until years later when he decided to become a writer. Joyce has written six books. His books have won awards and become best-sellers on Amazon. He now lives aboard a boat in Fort Lauderdale, Florida where he is busy working on his next book, tentatively entitled, *Mahoney*.

Other books by Andrew Joyce

Redemption: The Further Adventures of Huck Finn and Tom Sawyer

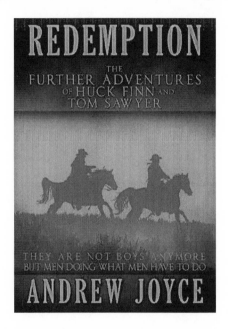

Winner of the 2013 Editors' Choice Award for Best Western

Three men come together in the town of Redemption Colorado, each for his own purpose.

Huck Finn is a famous lawman not afraid to use his gun to protect the weak. He has come to right a terrible wrong. After his wife's death, Tom Sawyer does not want to live anymore; he has come to die. The third man, the Laramie Kid, a killer Huck and Tom befriended years earlier, has come to kill a man. For these three men, Death is a constant companion.

For these three men it is their last chance for redemption.

Molly Lee

Molly is about to set off on the adventure of a lifetime ... of two lifetimes.

It's 1861 and the Civil War has just started. Molly is an eighteen-year-old girl living on her family's farm in Virginia when two deserters from the Southern Cause enter her life. One of them—a twenty-four-year-old Huck Finn—ends up saving her virtue, if not her life.

Molly is so enamored with Huck, she wants to run away with him. But Huck has other plans and is gone the next morning before she awakens. Thus starts a sequence of events that leads Molly into adventure after adventure; most of them not so nice. She starts off as a naive young girl. Over time, she develops into a strong, independent woman. The change is gradual. Her strengths come from the adversities she encounters along the road that is her life.

We follow the travails of Molly Lee, starting when she is eighteen and ending when she is fifty-three. Even then, Life has one more surprise in store for her.

Resolution: Huck Finn's Greatest Adventure

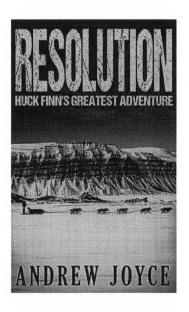

It is 1896 in the Yukon Territory, Canada. The largest gold strike in the annals of human history has just been made; however, word of the discovery will not reach the outside world for another year.

By happenstance, a fifty-nine-year-old Huck Finn and his lady friend, Molly Lee, are on hand, but they are not interested in gold. They have come to that neck of the woods seeking adventure.

Someone should have warned them, "Be careful what you wish for."

When disaster strikes, they volunteer to save the day by making an arduous six hundred mile journey by dog sled in the depths of a Yukon winter. They race against time, nature, and man. With the temperature hovering around seventy degrees below zero, they must fight every day if they are to live to see the next.

On the frozen trail, they are put upon by murderers, hungry wolves, and hostile Indians, but those adversaries have nothing over the weather. At seventy below, your spit freezes a foot from your face. Your cheeks burn--your skin turns purple and black as it dies from the cold. You are in constant danger of losing fingers and toes to frostbite.

It is into this world that Huck and Molly race.

They cannot stop or turn back. They can only go on. Lives hang in the balance—including theirs.

Yellow Hair

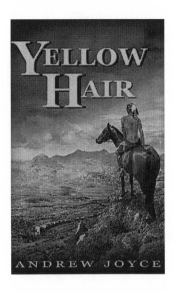

Awarded Book of the Year by Just Reviews.

Awarded Best Historical Fiction of 2016 by Colleen's Book Reviews.

Through no fault of his own, a young man is thrust into a new culture just at the time that culture is undergoing massive changes. It is losing its identity, its lands, and its dignity. He not only adapts, he perseveres and, over time, becomes a leader—and on occasion, the hand of vengeance against those who would destroy his adopted people.

Yellow Hair documents the injustices done to the Sioux Nation from their first treaty with the United States in 1805 through Wounded Knee in 1890. Every death, murder, battle, and outrage written about actually took place. The historical figures that play a role in this fact-based tale of fiction were real people and the author uses their real names. Yellow Hair is an epic tale of adventure, family, love, and hate that spans most of the 19th century.

This is American history.

Bedtime Stories for Grown-Ups

Bedtime Stories for Grown-ups is a jumble of genres—seven hundred pages of fiction and non-fiction ... some stories included against the author's better judgment. If he had known that one day they'd be published, he might not have been as honest when describing his past. Here is a tome of true stories about the author's criminal and misspent youth, historical accounts of the United

States when She was young, and tales of imagination encompassing every conceivable variety—all presented as though the author is sitting next to you at a bar and you're buying the drinks as long as he keeps coming up with captivating stories to hold your interest.

Made in the USA
Middletown, DE
18 June 2018